Table of Contents

Gift Giving Made Easy

Show your friends and family just how much you care by giving them a beautiful homemade gift jar filled with the ingredients to bake delicious muffins, breads and scones.

Keep the following tips in mind when preparing your gift jars:

- Always use a food-safe jar or container with an airtight lid. Make sure the jar or container is completely dry before filling it with ingredients.

- Use the jar size called for in the recipe.

- Measure all the ingredients accurately. Level off filled measuring cups with a metal spatula or knife.

- For ease in filling, use a wide mouth jar if possible. Layer the ingredients into the jar using a $\frac{1}{4}$-cup dry measuring cup or the largest spoon that fits through the mouth of the jar. Tightly pack each layer to insure that all ingredients fit into the jar.

- For more attractive jars, divide ingredients with large amounts (1 cup or more) into 2 layers.

- Fine ingredients such as flour and granulated sugar are best layered on the bottom of the jar, or on top of more compact ingredients, such as oats and brown sugar. When placed on top of loosely layered ingredients, such as chocolate chips or nuts, flour and granulated sugar tend to cover up those loosely layered ingredients.

- After the jar is filled, make sure to replace the lid securely. Write out the corresponding recipe on a decorative gift tag. Cover the top of the jar with a 9- or 10-inch circle of fabric. Tie the fabric and the gift tag onto the jar with raffia, ribbon, satin cord, string, yarn or lace.

Cookies, Bars & Brownies

MYSTICAL BARS MIX

- **1 cup graham cracker crumbs**
- **1 cup coarsely chopped pecans**
- **¾ cup flaked coconut**
- **¾ cup semisweet chocolate chips**
- **½ cup uncooked old-fashioned or quick oats**
- **½ cup raisins**

1. Layer ingredients attractively in any order into 1-quart food storage jar with tight-fitting lid. Pack ingredients down tightly before adding another layer.

2. Seal jar; cover top with fabric. Attach gift tag with raffia or ribbon.

Makes one 1-quart jar

MYSTICAL BARS

- **⅓ cup butter, melted**
- **1 jar Mystical Bars Mix**
- **1 can (14 ounces) sweetened condensed milk**

1. Preheat oven to 350°F. Pour butter into 13×9-inch baking pan.

continued on page 8

2. Place contents of jar in large bowl. Add sweetened condensed milk; stir with spoon until well blended.

3. Spread batter evenly in prepared pan. Bake 22 to 25 minutes or until lightly browned. Cool in pan on wire rack 5 minutes. Cut into bars. Cool completely in pan on wire rack. *Makes 2½ dozen bars*

COCOA AND PEANUT BUTTER YUMMY MIX
• • • • • • • • • • • • • • • •

½ **cup granulated sugar**
½ **cup brown sugar**
1⅓ **cups all-purpose flour**
¾ **teaspoon baking soda**
¼ **teaspoon salt**
½ **cup unsweetened cocoa**
1 **packages (12 ounces) peanut butter chips**

1. Layer ingredients in 1-quart wide -mouth canning jar in following order: granulated sugar; brown sugar, lightly packed; combined flour, baking soda and salt; cocoa; peanut butter chips.

2. Seal jar; cover top with fabric. Attach gift tag to jar with raffia or ribbon. *Makes one 1-quart jar*

COCOA AND PEANUT BUTTER YUMMIES

¾ cup (1½ sticks) butter
1 egg
2 tablespoons water
½ teaspoon vanilla
1 jar Cocoa and Peanut Butter Yummy Mix

1. Preheat oven to 375°F.

2. Beat butter in large bowl with electric mixer at medium speed until smooth. Beat in egg, water and vanilla. (Mixture may appear curdled.) Pour cookie mix into another large bowl; mix well. Stir into butter mixture until well blended.

3. Drop dough by rounded tablespoonfuls 3 inches apart onto cookie sheets.

4. Bake 8 to 10 minutes or until firm in center. *Do not overbake.* Remove to wire racks to cool. *Makes about 4 dozen cookies*

Cookies, Bars & Brownies

HAPPY BIRTHDAY COOKIE MIX

1¼ cups flour
½ teaspoon baking powder
¼ teaspoon baking soda
¼ teaspoon salt
⅓ cup packed brown sugar
⅓ cup granulated sugar
½ cup chocolate-covered toffee chips
¾ cup mini candy-coated chocolate pieces
½ cup peanut butter and milk chocolate chips
½ cup lightly salted peanuts, coarsely chopped

1. Combine flour, baking soda, baking powder and salt in large bowl. Spoon flour mixture into 1-quart food storage jar with tight-fitting lid. Layer remaining ingredients on top of flour. Pack ingredients down lightly before adding another layer.

2. Seal jar; cover top with fabric. Attach gift tag to jar with raffia or ribbon. *Makes one 1-quart jar*

HAPPY BIRTHDAY COOKIES

½ cup (1 stick) butter, softened
1 egg
½ teaspoon vanilla
1 jar Happy Birthday Cookie Mix

1. Preheat oven to 375°F. Line cookie sheets with parchment paper.

2. Beat butter in large bowl until fluffy. Beat in egg and vanilla. Add contents of jar to butter mixture; beat 1 minute or until light dough forms.

3. Drop dough by rounded tablespoonfuls 2 inches apart onto prepared cookie sheets. Bake 10 minutes or until firm and light brown. Let cookies stand 1 minute. Remove to wire racks to cool completely.

Makes 3 dozen cookies

Cookies, Bars & Brownies

Fudgy Chocolate-Amaretti Brownie Mix

$^2/_3$ cup unsweetened cocoa powder
1 cup all-purpose flour
1 teaspoon baking powder
$^1/_4$ teaspoon salt
$^1/_2$ cup amaretti cookie crumbs
$^3/_4$ cup granulated sugar
$^1/_2$ cup packed brown sugar
$^1/_2$ cup semisweet chocolate chips
$^1/_3$ cup powdered sugar

1. Layer all ingredients except powdered sugar in order as listed above in 1-quart food storage jar with tight-fitting lid. Lightly pack down ingredients before adding another layer. Place powdered sugar in small plastic food storage bag. Close with twist tie; cut off top of bag. Place bag in jar.

2. Seal jar; cover top with fabric. Attach gift tag with raffia or ribbon.

Makes one 1-quart jar

Fudgy Chocolate-Amaretti Brownies

1 jar Fudgy Chocolate-Amaretti Brownie Mix
$^1/_2$ cup (1 stick) butter, softened
1 teaspoon vanilla
2 eggs
2 tablespoons almond-flavored liqueur or milk
   Holiday-shaped stencil or doily with large pattern

1. Preheat oven to 350°F. Grease 9-inch square baking pan.

2. Remove powdered sugar from jar. Place remaining contents of jar in large bowl; stir until well blended. Beat butter and vanilla in separate bowl with electric mixer on medium speed until smooth, Beat in eggs and liqueur. (Mixture may appear curdled.) Add butter mixture to flour mixture; stir until well blended.

3. Spoon batter into prepared pan. Press down with back of spoon. (Batter will be thick and sticky. It will spread out during baking.) Bake 20 to 25 minutes or until brownies spring back when lightly touched. Do not overbake. Cool in pan on wire rack.

4. Store, covered, in refrigerator for fudgy brownies. Before serving, place stencil on top of brownies. Dust with powdered sugar; remove stencil. Cut into bars. *Makes about 1½ dozen brownies*

Cookies, Bars & Brownies

TRIPLE CHIP COOKIE MIX

- ½ **cup granulated sugar**
- 1 **cup packed light brown sugar**
- 2½ **cups all-purpose flour**
- 1 **teaspoon baking soda**
- ¾ **teaspoon salt**
- 2 **cups semisweet chocolate chips**
- ½ **cup white chocolate chips**
- ½ **cup butterscotch or peanut butter chips**

1. Layer ingredients in 2-quart wide-mouth canning jar in following order: granulated sugar; brown sugar, lightly packed; combined flour, baking soda and salt; chocolate chips; white chocolate chips; butterscotch chips.

2. Seal jar; cover top with fabric. Attach gift tag to jar with raffia or ribbon. *Makes one 2-quart jar*

TRIPLE CHIP COOKIES

- 1 **cup (2 sticks) butter, softened**
- 2 **eggs**
- 2 **teaspoons vanilla**
- 1 **jar Triple Chip Cookie Mix**

1. Preheat oven to 375°F.

2. Beat butter in large bowl with electric mixer until smooth. Add eggs, one at a time, beating well after each addition. Beat in vanilla. Pour cookie mix into another large bowl and mix well. Stir into butter mixture until well blended.

3. Drop dough by scant ⅛ cupfuls onto ungreased cookie sheets, spacing 3 inches apart. Lightly flatten dough with fingertips. Bake 12 to 14 minutes or until edges are set and light brown. Cool cookies 1 to 2 minutes on cookie sheets; transfer to wire racks. Cool completely.

Makes about 3 dozen cookies

Cookies, Bars & Brownies

Breads & Muffins

BANANA CHOCOLATE MINI MUFFIN MIX

2¼ cups all-purpose flour
1 cup packed brown sugar
1 cup mini chocolate-coated candy pieces or mini chocolate chips
2 teaspoons baking powder
½ teaspoon salt

1. Layer ingredients attractively in any order into 1-quart food storage jar with tight-fitting lid. Pack ingredients down tightly before adding another layer.

2. Seal jar; cover top with fabric. Attach gift tag with raffia or ribbon.

Makes one 1-quart jar

BANANA CHOCOLATE MINI MUFFINS

1 jar Banana Chip Mini Muffin Mix
1 cup mashed ripe bananas (about 2 large)
½ cup (1 stick) butter, melted
2 eggs
½ teaspoon vanilla

1. Preheat oven to 350°F. Grease or paper-line 36 mini (1¾-inch) muffin cups.

continued on page 18

16

2. Pour contents of jar into large bowl. Beat bananas, butter, eggs and vanilla in medium bowl with electric mixer until blended; stir into jar mixture just until moistened. Spoon evenly into prepared muffin cups, filling almost full.

3. Bake about 15 minutes or until tops are golden brown and toothpick inserted into centers comes out clean. Cool in pans on wire racks 5 minutes; remove from pans and cool completely on wire racks.

Makes 36 mini muffins

CRANBERRY-RAISIN BREAD MIX

2¼ cups cake flour
1 cup granulated sugar
1½ teaspoons baking powder
¼ teaspoon salt
1 cup dried cranberries
½ cup chopped macadamia nuts, toasted*
¾ cup dark raisins
¾ cup golden raisins

*To toast macadamia nuts, preheat oven to 350°F. Spread nuts on ungreased baking sheet. Bake 5 to 7 minutes, stirring occasionally, or until brown.

1. Whisk together flour, sugar, baking powder and salt in a medium mixing bowl. Layer mixture into 1-quart jar with tight-fitting lid a third at one time, packing down firmly before adding next layer. Layer remaining ingredients in the following order: cranberries; macadamia nuts; dark raisins and golden raisins, packing down firmly before adding next layer.

2. Seal jar; cover top with fabric. Attach gift tag with raffia or ribbon.

Makes one 1-quart jar

CRANBERRY-RAISIN BREAD

1 jar Cranberry-Raisin Bread Mix
¾ cup orange juice
Zest from 1 orange (about 1 tablespoon)
1 egg
3 tablespoons corn or vegetable oil

1. Preheat oven to 350°F. Spray 9×5×3-inch loaf pan with nonstick cooking spray.

2. Place contents of jar in large bowl; stir to evenly distribute dried fruit and nuts. Add orange juice, zest, egg and oil; stir just until moistened.

3. Spread batter evenly in prepared pan. Bake 50 to 60 minutes or until toothpick inserted into center comes out clean. Let bread rest in pan 10 minutes; place on wire rack to cool. *Makes 1 loaf*

Breads & Muffins

19

CRANBERRY CORN BREAD MIX

1½ cups all-purpose flour
1 cup yellow cornmeal
1 cup dried cranberries
½ cup sugar
2 teaspoons baking powder
½ teaspoon baking soda
½ teaspoon salt

1. Layer ingredients attractively in any order in 1-quart food storage jar with tight-fitting lid. Pack ingredients down lightly before adding another layer.

2. Seal jar; cover top with fabric. Attach gift tag with raffia or ribbon.

Makes one 1-quart jar

CRANBERRY CORN BREAD

1 jar Cranberry Corn Bread Mix
½ cup shortening
1⅓ cups buttermilk
2 eggs

1. Preheat oven to 350°F. Spray 8½×4½-inch loaf pan with nonstick cooking spray.

2. Pour contents of jar into large bowl. Cut in shortening with pastry blender or two knives until mixture resembles coarse crumbs. Beat buttermilk and eggs in small bowl until blended. Add to shortening mixture; stir until mixture forms stiff batter. (Batter will be lumpy.) Pour into prepared pan, spreading evenly and removing any air bubbles.

3. Bake 45 to 50 minutes or until toothpick inserted into center comes out clean. Cool in pan on wire rack 10 minutes; remove from pan and cool 10 minutes longer. Serve warm.

Makes 1 loaf

Breads & Muffins

Soups, Chilis & Snacks

ALPHABET SOUP IN MINUTES MIX

1 1/4 cups uncooked alphabet pasta
2 tablespoons dried vegetable flakes or soup greens (see note page 24)
1 teaspoon chicken bouillon granules
1/8 teaspoon black pepper
1/2 cup small fish-shaped or cheese crackers

1. Layer 3/4 cup pasta, vegetable flakes, bouillon granules, pepper and remaining 1/2 cup pasta in 1-pint food storage jar with tight-fitting lid. Place crackers into small food storage bag. Close bag with twist tie and cut off top of bag. Place bag on top of pasta.

2. Seal jar; cover top with fabric. Attach gift tag with raffia or ribbon.

Makes one 1-pint jar

ALPHABET SOUP IN MINUTES

1 jar Alphabet Soup in Minutes Mix
4 cups water
1/4 cup pasta sauce

1. Remove crackers from jar; set aside.

2. Place water, pasta sauce and remaining contents of jar into large saucepan. Bring to a boil over high heat; reduce heat and simmer 10 minutes, uncovered, or until alphabets are tender. Serve with crackers.

Makes 4 to 5 servings

Italian Tomato and Pasta Soup Mix

·······················

2½ cups farfalle (bow tie) or rotini pasta
2 tablespoons dried vegetable flakes, soup greens or dehydrated
    vegetables (see note)
1 tablespoon dried minced onion
1 teaspoon chicken bouillon granules
1 teaspoon Italian herb seasoning
1 teaspoon sugar
½ teaspoon dried minced garlic
¼ teaspoon black pepper
½ cup grated Parmesan cheese

1. Place pasta in 1-quart food storage jar with tight-fitting lid. Add
vegetable flakes, onion, bouillon granules, Italian seasoning, sugar, garlic
and pepper. Shake jar to mix seasoning. Place Parmesan cheese in small
food storage bag. Close with twist tie and cut off top of bag. Place bag on
top of pasta.

2. Seal jar; cover top with fabric. Attach gift tag with raffia or ribbon.

Makes one 1-quart jar

Note: Vegetable Flakes and Soup Greens made by McCORMICK® are
available in the spice section of large supermarkets. If these products are
not available, ask your grocer to order them. Also, look for dried vegetable
flakes (bell peppers, carrots, etc.) in the bulk food section of specialty food
markets such as natural or bulk food stores.

ITALIAN TOMATO AND PASTA SOUP

1 jar Italian Tomato and Pasta Soup Mix
5 cups water
1 can (28 ounces) crushed tomatoes, undrained
½ package (10 ounces) frozen chopped spinach, thawed
4 to 6 slices crisp-cooked bacon, crumbled

1. Remove cheese packet from jar; set aside.

2. Combine water and remaining contents of jar in large saucepan. Bring to a boil over hight heat; boil 10 to 12 minutes. Stir in tomatoes with juice, spinach and bacon. Reduce heat; simmer 10 to 12 minutes or until pasta is tender. Serve with Parmesan cheese.   *Makes 4 to 5 servings*

Note: 3 cups chopped fresh spinach, rinsed and stemmed can be substituted for frozen spinach.

Spicy Chili Mac Mix

¾ **cup dried pinto beans**
¾ **cup dried red kidney beans**
 1 **package (about 1¼ ounces) chili seasoning mix**
 2 **tablespoons dried minced onion**
 2 **teaspoons beef bouillon granules**
¼ **teaspoon red pepper flakes**
1½ **cups uncooked rotini pasta**

1. Layer pinto and kidney beans in 1-quart food storage jar with tight-fitting lid. Combine chili seasoning, onion, bouillon granules and pepper flakes in small food storage bag. Close bag with twist tie and place on top of beans spreading out bag to cover beans. Add pasta.

2. Seal jar; cover top with fabric. Attach gift tag with raffia or ribbon.

Makes one 1-quart jar

Spicy Chili Mac

 1 **jar Spicy Chili Mac Mix**
 4 **to 5 cups water**
 2 **cans (14½ ounces) diced tomatoes with green chiles, undrained**
 1 **pound ground beef or ground turkey, browned and drained**
   Shredded Cheddar cheese (optional)

1. Remove pasta and seasoning packet from jar; set aside. Place beans in large bowl; cover with water. Soak 6 to 8 hours or overnight. (To quick soak beans, place beans in large saucepan; cover with water. Bring to a boil over high heat. Boil 2 minutes. Remove from heat; let soak, covered, 1 hour.) Drain beans; discard water.

2. Combine soaked beans, water, tomatoes with juice, ground beef and contents of seasoning packet in Dutch oven. Bring to a boil over high heat. Cover; reduce heat and simmer 1½ hours. Add pasta and simmer 30 to 45 minutes. Sprinkle with Cheddar cheese, if desired.

Makes 8 to 10 servings

Soups, Chilis & Snacks

LAYERED BEAN SOUP MIX

½ cup dried black beans
½ cup dried white beans
½ cup green split peas
½ cup dried pink or red beans
½ cup dried pinto beans
½ cup dried lentils
½ cup dried black-eyed peas
¼ cup dried chopped or minced onion
¼ cup dried parsley flakes
1 teaspoon garlic powder
1 teaspoon dried basil
6 vegetable bouillon cubes, unwrapped
2 whole bay leaves

1. Layer beans, peas and lentils in 1-quart jar with tight-fitting lid. Combine onion, parsley flakes, garlic powder and basil in small bowl; place in resealable food storage bag with bouillon and bay leaves. Close bag with twist tie and cut off top. Place bag in jar.

2. Seal jar; cover top with fabric; attach gift tag with raffia or ribbon.

Makes one 1-quart jar

LAYERED BEAN SOUP

1 jar Layered Bean Soup Mix
8 cups water
Chopped tomatoes, chopped cilantro, grated mozzarella cheese, sour cream or plain yogurt for garnish (optional)

1. Remove seasoning packet from jar. Place beans in 5- to 6-quart pot; add enough water to cover by 1 inch. Bring to a boil over high heat; reduce heat and simmer, covered, 5 minutes. Turn off heat and let beans sit, covered, for 1 hour; drain.

Soups, Chilis & Snacks

2. Add 8 cups water and contents of seasoning packet. Bring to a boil over high heat, cover, and reduce heat; simmer 90 minutes or until beans are tender.

3. Remove 1 cup soup to a bowl, and mash with a fork. Return mashed beans to pot and simmer, uncovered, 30 minutes, stirring occasionally. Remove bay leaves. Garnish each serving as desired.

Makes 8 servings

SWEET & SPICY SNACK MIX

  3 cups popped corn
2½ cups miniature
  1 cup pecan halves or pistachio nuts
  ⅓ cup packed brown sugar
  ½ teaspoon ground cinnamon
  ¼ teaspoon ground red pepper

1. Layer popped corn, pretzels and pecans in any order in 2-quart food storage jar with tight-fitting lid. Place brown sugar, cinnamon and red pepper in small food storage bag. Close bag with twist tie. Cut off top of bag. Place in jar.

2. Seal jar; cover top with fabric. Attach gift tag with raffia or ribbon.

Makes one 2-quart jar

SWEET & SPICY SNACK MIX

  1 jar Sweet & Spicy Snack Mix
  ¼ cup (½ stick) butter

Remove seasoning packet from jar. Place butter and contents of seasoning packet in 4-quart microwaveble bowl. Microwave on HIGH 1½ minutes or until bubbly. Remove from oven; stir in remaining contents of jar; mixing well. Microwave on HIGH 1 to 2 minutes. Remove and stir to coat mixture evenly. Cool completely. *Makes 6 cups snack mix*

Soups, Chilis & Snacks **31**

TACO BEAN CHILI MIX

½ cup dried kidney beans
½ cup dried pinto beans
½ cup dried red beans
1 package (1¼ ounces) taco seasoning mix
1 tablespoon dried minced onion
½ teaspoon chili powder or chipotle chili pepper seasoning
¼ teaspoon ground cumin
1½ cups tortilla chips, slightly crushed

1. Layer kidney beans, pinto beans and red beans in 1-quart food storage jar with tight-fitting lid. Place taco seasoning mix, onion, chili powder and cumin in small food storage bag. Close with twist tie and cut off top of bag. Place in jar spreading out to cover beans. Add tortilla chips.

2. Seal jar; cover top with fabric. Attach gift tag with raffia or ribbon.

Makes one 1-quart jar

TACO BEAN CHILI

1 jar Taco Bean Chili Mix
4 cups water
1 can (14½ ounces) diced tomatoes with green chiles, undrained
1 can (8 ounces) tomato sauce
1 pound ground beef or ground turkey, browned and drained
    Shredded cheese, chopped lettuce, sliced black olives (optional)

1. Remove chips and seasoning packet from jar; set aside.

2. Place beans in large bowl; cover with water. Soak 6 to 8 hours or overnight. (To quick soak beans, place beans in large saucepan; cover with water. Bring to a boil over high heat. Boil 2 minutes. Remove from heat; let soak, covered, 1 hour.) Drain beans; discard water.

3. Place soaked beans, water, tomatoes with juice, tomato sauce, ground beef and contents of seasoning packet in Dutch oven. Bring to a boil over high heat. Cover; reduce heat and simmer 1½ to 2 hours or until beans are tender.

4. Crush tortilla chips. Stir into chili and cook 5 to 10 minutes to thicken. Serve with cheese, lettuce and olives, if desired.

Makes 6 to 8 servings

Tip: Make a taco salad with leftover chili.

Kids' Treats

BEAR BITE SNACK MIX

1½ cups sweetened corn or oat cereal squares
1 cup raisins
1 cup teddy bear-shaped cookies
½ cup dried fruit bits or chopped mixed dried fruit

1. Layer ingredients in 1-quart food storage jar with tight-fitting lid in following order: cereal; cookies; fruit; and raisins in small plastic bag.

2. Seal jar; cover top with fabric. Attach gift tag to jar with raffia or ribbon.   *Makes one 1-quart jar*

BEAR BITE SNACK MIX

2 teaspoons sugar
¾ teaspoon ground cinnamon
¼ teaspoon ground nutmeg
1 jar Bear Bite Snack Mix
Nonstick cooking spray

1. Preheat oven to 350°F. Combine sugar, cinnamon and nutmeg in small bowl; mix well.

2. Place contents of jar on jelly-roll pan. Generously spray with cooking spray. Sprinkle with half sugar mixture. Stir well. Spray again with cooking spray; sprinkle with remaining sugar mixture. Bake 5 minutes; stir. Bake 5 minutes more; stir. Cool completely in pan on wire rack. Store in airtight container.   *Makes 4 cups snack mix*

BANANA SNACK CAKE MIX

1¼ cups all-purpose flour
1 cup semisweet chocolate chips
¾ cup packed brown sugar
½ cup granulated sugar
½ cup chopped walnuts
1 teaspoon baking powder
¾ teaspoon salt
½ teaspoon baking soda

1. Layer ingredients attractively in any order in 1-quart food storage jar with tight-fitting lid. Pack ingredients down lightly before adding another layer.

2. Seal jar; cover top with fabric. Attach gift tag to jar with raffia or ribbon.   *Makes one 1-quart jar*

BANANA SNACK CAKE

1 jar Banana Snack Cake Mix
1¼ cups mashed ripe bananas (about 4 medium)
½ cup vegetable oil
2 eggs, beaten
1 teaspoon vanilla

1. Preheat oven to 350°F. Grease and flour 8- or 9-inch square baking pan.

2. Place contents of jar in large bowl. Add bananas, oil, eggs and vanilla; stir until well blended. Pour into prepared pan.

3. Bake 40 to 45 minutes or until toothpick inserted into center comes out clean. Cool completely in pan on wire rack.

Makes 9 to 12 servings

Banana Snack Cake

1 jar Banana Snack Cake Mix
1¼ cups mashed ripe bananas
(about 4 medium)
½ cup vegetable oil
2 eggs, beaten
1 teaspoon vanilla
Chocolate frosting

1. Preheat oven to 350°F. Grease and flour 9×9-inch baking
pan well Baked. Pour in coated pan.
2. Place contents of jar in large bowl. Add banana, oil
until well blended.
1. Bake 40 to 45 minutes.
Cool completely in pan.

EASY LAYERED BAR MIX

½ cup candy-coated chocolate candy or baking bits
1 cup semisweet chocolate chips
1¼ cups crisp rice cereal
1 cup peanut butter chips
½ cup coconut
1½ cups graham cracker crumbs

1. Layer ingredients in 1½-quart food storage jar with tight-fitting lid in following order: candy; chocolate chips; cereal; peanut butter chips; coconut; and graham cracker crumbs in small plastic bag.

2. Seal jar; cover top with fabric. Attach gift tag to jar with raffia or ribbon. *Makes one 1½-quart jar*

EASY LAYERED BARS

½ cup (1 stick) butter or margarine, melted
1 can (14 ounces) sweetened condensed milk
1 jar Easy Layered Bar Mix

1. Preheat oven to 350°F. Lightly spray sides of 13×9-inch baking pan with nonstick cooking spray. Pour butter into pan.

2. Remove graham cracker crumbs from jar and sprinkle over butter. Pour condensed milk evenly over crumbs. Carefully sprinkle coconut and peanut butter chips in even layers, then cereal, chocolate chips and baking bits; press gently.

3. Bake 25 to 27 minutes or until top just begins to brown. Cool completely in pan on wire rack. Cut into bars. *Makes about 36 bars*

Happy Holidays

CRISPY HOLIDAY TREATS MIX

　1 cup powdered sugar
1½ cups crisp rice cereal
　½ cup chopped dried tart cherries
　¾ cup mini semisweet chocolate chips
　¼ cup chopped toasted pecans
　¾ cup flaked coconut

1. Layer all ingredients except coconut in the order listed above in 1-quart food storage jar with tight-fitting lid. Pack ingredients down firmly before adding another layer. Place coconut in small plastic food storage bag. Close with twist tie; cut off top of bag. Place bag in jar.

2. Seal jar; cover top with fabric. Attach gift tag with raffia or ribbon.

Makes one 1-quart jar

Gift Idea: Assemble a holiday gift bag with a jar of Crispy Holiday Treats Mix, a package of small-size paper or foil candy cups and a decorative candy dish.

continued on page 42

Crispy Holiday Treats

1 jar Crispy Holiday Treats Mix
1 cup creamy butter
¼ cup butter softened

1. Remove coconut from jar. Place remaining co. ll co of jar into b.
mix well. Beat together peanut bu and butter edium bo
combined. Add to cereal mixture; mix well.

2. Shape teaspoonfuls of mixture into h ball
in food storage container. Refrigerate 1 h

CRISPY HOLIDAY TREATS

• •

1 jar Crispy Holiday Treats Mix
1 cup peanut butter
¼ cup (½ stick) butter, softened

1. Remove coconut packet from jar. Place remaining contents of jar in large bowl; stir to blend. Combine peanut butter and butter in medium bowl, stirring until well blended. Add to cereal mixture. Stir until well blended.

2. Shape rounded teaspoonfuls of dough into 1½-inch balls. Roll balls in coconut. Place in single layer in large food storage container. Store in refrigerator.   *Makes about 2 dozen treats*

SNOWY DATE NUT SQUARES MIX

• •

1¼ cups all-purpose flour
1 teaspoon dried orange peel
½ teaspoon baking powder
¼ teaspoon baking soda
¼ teaspoon salt
¼ teaspoon ground cinnamon
¼ teaspoon ground nutmeg
⅛ teaspoon ground cloves
1½ cups (8 ounces) finely chopped dates
¼ cup packed brown sugar
¼ cup granulated sugar
½ cup finely chopped toasted* walnuts
1 cup powdered sugar

*Place nuts in a microwavable dish. Microwave on HIGH 1 to 2 minutes or just until light golden brown, stirring nuts every 30 seconds. Allow to stand 3 minutes. Cool completely.

1. Layer all ingredients except powdered sugar in the order listed above in wide mouth 1-quart food storage jar with tight-fitting lid. Lightly pack down ingredients before adding another layer. Place powdered sugar in small plastic food storage bag. Close with twist tie; cut off top of bag. Place bag in jar.

2. Seal jar; cover top with fabric. Attach gift tag with raffia or ribbon.

Makes one 1-quart jar

SNOWY DATE NUT SQUARES

1 jar Snowy Date Nut Squares Mix
½ cup (1 stick) butter, softened
2 eggs
2 tablespoons orange juice

1. Preheat oven to 350°F. Spray 8-inch square baking pan with nonstick cooking spray.

2. Remove powdered sugar packet from jar. Pour remaining contents of jar into large bowl; stir until well blended. Beat butter in medium bowl with electric mixer on medium speed until smooth. Beat in eggs, one at a time. (Mixture may appear curdled.) Beat in orange juice. Add butter mixture to date-nut mixture; stir until well blended. Spread batter into prepared pan.

3. Bake 25 to 30 minutes or until toothpick inserted into center comes out clean. Cool slightly in pan on wire rack; cut into 1-inch squares. Place powdered sugar in small bowl. Roll warm cookies in powdered sugar, coating well.

Makes 36 (1-inch) squares

LUSCIOUS ORANGE-CRANBERRY SCONE MIX

- 1 cup all-purpose flour
- ¾ cup dried cranberries or dried blueberries
- ½ cup packed brown sugar
- ¼ cup granulated sugar
- 1 cup all-purpose flour
- 2 teaspoons baking powder
- ½ teaspoon ground ginger
- ½ teaspoon ground cinnamon
- ¼ teaspoon baking soda
- ¼ teaspoon salt
- ½ cup powdered sugar

1. Layer all ingredients except powdered sugar in order listed above in 1-quart food storage jar with tight-fitting lid. Pack ingredients down frimly before adding another layer. Place powdered sugar in small plastic food storage bag. Close with twist tie; cut off top of bag. Place bag in jar.

2. Seal jar; cover top with fabric. Attach gift tag with raffia or ribbon.

Makes one 1-quart jar

Luscious Lemon Blueberry Scones: Substitute dried blueberries for cranberries in the jar mix. Use lemon flavors when preparing scones.

LUSCIOUS ORANGE-CRANBERRY SCONES

- 1 jar Luscious Orange-Cranberry Scones Mix
- 6 tablespoons (¾ stick) butter, cut into pieces and softened
- ½ cup buttermilk
- 1 egg
- 2 teaspoons grated orange or lemon peel
- 1 teaspoon orange or lemon extract
- 2 to 3 teaspoons orange or lemon juice

1. Preheat oven to 350°F. Lightly grease baking sheet.

2. Remove powdered sugar from jar. Place remaining contents of jar in large bowl. Cut in butter with pastry blender or two knives until mixture resembles coarse crumbs. Whisk together buttermilk, egg, orange peel and orange extract in small bowl. Add buttermilk mixture to flour mixture; stir until stiff dough is formed. Knead dough in bowl. Drop by ¼ cupfuls onto prepared baking sheet.

3. Bake 18 to 20 minutes or until toothpick inserted into centers comes out clean. Remove to wire racks; cool 10 minutes. Stir together powdered sugar and enough orange juice to make glaze. Drizzle over scones. Serve warm. *Makes 12 scones*

TANGY LEMONADE BAR MIX

2¼ **cups all-purpose flour**
1 **cup sugar**
1 **cup dried cranberries**
1 **tablespoon grated lemon peel**
¾ **teaspoon baking soda**
¾ **teaspoon salt**

1. Layer ingredients attractively in any order into 1½-quart food storage jar with tight-fitting lid. Pack ingredients down lightly before adding another layer.

2. Seal jar; cover top with fabric. Attach gift tag with raffia or ribbon.

Makes one 1½-quart jar

TANGY LEMONADE BARS

½ **cup butter, softened**
⅓ **cup thawed frozen lemonade concentrate**
1 **egg**
1 **jar Tangy Lemonade Bars Mix**

1. Preheat oven to 375°F. Lightly grease 13×9-inch baking pan.

2. Beat butter in large bowl until smooth. Beat in lemonade concentrate and egg until blended. (Mixture may appear curdled.) Add bar cookie mix to butter mixture; stir until well blended.

3. Press dough evenly in prepared pan. Bake 20 to 25 minutes or until light brown. Cool completely in pan on wire rack. Cut into bars.

Makes 2½ dozen bars